How to *Survive* Homeschooling

A SELF-CARE GUIDE FOR MOMS
WHO LOVINGLY DO WAY TOO MUCH

BROOKE BENOIT

First Edition, 2018

Copyright 2018 How to Survive Homeschooling
www.brookebenoit.com
Written by Brooke Benoit

Design by Reyhana Ismail
www.reyoflightdesign.com

ACKNOWLEDGMENTS

Thank you so much to my mother, Sandie Benoit, who has always supported my creative endeavors and unconventional decisions. Being the child of a black sheep has come with many, many perks! My longtime friend and best editor ever, Aaminah Shakur, thank you for reminding me every year or so that I should write a book like this. And thank you to my children who had nothing but words of encouragement when I went on a one-month retreat to finish this manuscript.

"A truly good person will speak truth, act with truth, and stand for Truth. *A truly good person is not afraid to think from their heart; therefore, allowing nonconformist decisions, viewpoints, and perspectives to lead their life. By following their heart, they stand with their conscience, and only with God."*

- Suzy Kassem

"Surround yourself with people that want more out of life. That won't settle for average. People that you can connect with on a deeper level. Keep your circle fresh. Keep your circle full of quality rather than quantity. Full of cool ass humans that you can be yourself around. People that fill you up with nothing but love. People that want to see you succeed. People that GET IT. Good circle, good life!"

-Genereux Philip

CONTENTS

INTRODUCTION

I have written this book as a source of inspiration and support for homeschooling moms, who I believe are doing some of the hardest emotional work on the planet. In addition to homeschooling my seven children for over fifteen years, I was also homeschooled for my last year of high school. Because of my long-time status as a homeschooler, many people have suggested that I write a book about my experiences. I can see how that makes sense as I am both a writer and a homeschooler, but I simply could not see what kind of book I would write. I certainly can't write a how-to-homeschool since I know that it is a fully unique experience for each family; there is simply no one way, and my own children have used multiple homeschooling styles and resources. I also couldn't write a memoir as my family is still immersed in the process, and I believe the end result is really what people would want to read in there. Though I have no idea how it will turn out for any of my children, I am thrilled to report that my eldest has graduated the high school phase and two of his siblings are actively studying for their SATS (Scholastic Assessment Test for college admissions). So how then can I best help the many people turning to me for information and support?

I find that practical information on homeschooling is easy enough to find through your favorite search engine or at a larger library. Libraries that do interlibrary loans from other libraries are heavenly! Ask your librarian about such things if you don't already know. But this area - the curriculum and how-to phase - quickly becomes a black hole, devouring us in the search for the ultimate way to homeschool our children. That pursuit alone becomes all encompassing, often taking over our lives for a year or so, then again when we decide to try something else, and when another child has a different style. When we have a fairly firm hold on curriculum or at least style, then there are the details to further suck us in. See, I can't tell you how to do it. If you haven't already, you'll just have to look at all the options and try the one(s) that makes the most sense to your family.

6

PROTIP: This period of exploration can be cut short if you are freaked out about rushing to get started so that your children don't fall behind. You can stop worrying and trust the experiences of millions of other homeschoolers. Homeschooled children are nearly always ahead of their contemporaries in one area or another. *Deschool* yourself and your child(ren) during this exploratory time. Deschooling is essentially rethinking how you approach education outside of an institutionalized setting. Instead of recreating a school at home, slow down, shrug off some of that school trauma and residue that both you and your child have. Communicate openly with your child and envision together how you will acquire their optimal education.

After you have found a homeschooling style, curriculum, etc., then new homeschoolers usually get into the nitty gritty of how to hands-on do all these things, such as organizing your homeschooling space(s), finding crafts and specific activities that are old hand to seasoned teachers. "Look on Pinterest!" other homeschooling mamas sweetly suggest, and several hours later you have accomplished nothing and feel bad about yourself for not being as creative/organised/motherly as all those homeschool blogger moms. Blogger Moms are the Soccer Moms of the 21st century. Do not let them make you feel bad! Use their inspiration in small doses and carry on. It is this "feeling bad stuff" that I am here to obliterate for you. Again, you are doing amazing things for and with your children. Make that your mantra and scream it in the face of anyone who dares to question you: "I AM DOING AMAZING THINGS FOR MY CHILDREN."

[handwritten margin note: Yes! No feeling bad!]

Finding the emotional support to homeschool is much more elusive than the material goods. Not only can homeschooling support be hard to get, but it also erratically ebbs and flows, frequently leaving us feeling very isolated in this work. Spouses, partners, family members, friends, exes, and others can easily take it for granted that we have everything covered while they simply have no idea of the immense span of work we are doing. Frankly, many men see homeschooling as just another task that

Domestic work should be shared by all in the household.

can be folded into a mom's already unfair load of domestic work. And I suspect many women fear discussing this disproportion of workload because they don't want their husbands to suggest throwing in the towel, which would be easier for them than actually getting down in the mud or finger painting alongside their wives. So who then can we turn to?

Homeschooling moms, though truly the soundest source of support via their firsthand experiences, are ridiculously busy and rapidly moving through countless stages of their own lives. Fair enough, their support is often here one day, gone tomorrow; many have their kids in and out of school, physically move homes, go through their own periods of struggle and even depression. Take whatever you can and give back in fair measure. Ultimately you will be your own best source of support.

Do not let yourself be all engrossed in the newness and energy you *think* getting a handle on homeschooling needs. It can and will take every drop of energy from you if you let it. You have to pace yourself and take care of yourself, or else you can easily lose yourself in this process that can take 12+ years of your *life*. You don't have to and should not give your child too much of your own time and life. If you bought this book, then you have an inkling about the importance of carving out time yourself along this journey. And if this book was gifted to you- wonderful! You already have a good ally at your side.

While I offer my own stories in this book to inspire and entertain you, I have primarily made it an exercise and record-keeping journal style so that you can become your own best support. Here you can write down important things you don't want to forget, have records of successes to help lift you in dark times and to celebrate as you go along (as we should), leave patterns so you can remember what to avoid or try differently next time, and maybe even become a better support to that next homeschooling mom who slides up to you.

In my experience, I have found homeschooling moms to be at the highest levels of self-sacrificing. Nearly everything you are doing in your life is for your children, but when you have given your absolute all, then what is left of you to further give? This is basic arithmetic - giving all without replenishing leaves nothing. Your children won't appreciate an exhausted, burnt out martyr of a mom. They will resent you or take you for granted, becoming bitter or entitled people. That isn't what you want to "achieve" by homeschooling, is it? Please use this book to maintain and regain your serenity, to highlight the joy, and keep your eye on the prize.

PART ONE:
Your Surviving And Thriving Guide

CHAPTER ONE:
POUR YOUR FOUNDATION HERE

"Don't say 'I need diapers,' because you don't. Say 'The baby needs diapers' because she does." This is a snippet of advice I once heard about communicating with your spouse about finances. Apparently this is a common problem for families; a woman's needs and those of the household are lumped together, so that women feel guilty about asking for their specific needs. After all, they ask for/need so much if they don't separate these things out. Women are often the primary shopper in households and they need groceries, household supplies, home and car repairs done, new clothes for growing children, and so on. They spend an awful lot of money, don't they? I immediately saw how this dynamic was playing out in my homeschooling family. I didn't need reams of paper and gas to get to all of the kids activities around town. I didn't need a full wall-sized bookcase to house all of our books and supplies. *These were things the homeschool needed.* I began to see our homeschool similar to a business, with specific tasks and supplies needed to run it. This was very freeing for me in many ways and helpful to better plan and budget rather than feel guilty about everything I was purchasing. Another practical tip came along a few years later.

Surely you've heard of businesses and other endeavors writing mission, vision, and even value statements? Have you done one? Even though I saw my homeschool as a business of sorts, and I regularly remind other moms that they are running a business, I didn't write these up myself until about fifteen years into my homeschooling journey when I read homeschool blogger Priscilla Martinez's suggestion to do so. Prior to that I inwardly clung to a morphed version of a mission and vision globbed together. Don't do that. Mission and vision are two different things and at least one will likely evolve during your homeschooling years. Writing down these statements, revisiting, and revising them are hugely rewarding to maintain your steadfastness. I loved the way doing an actual mission and vision refocused me and am sure you will too.

Return to these at least every six months or when you are feeling adrift, tangled, hopeless, and/or smashy. Read your mission and vision statements, take a moment to remember why you are doing this homeschooling thing, recommit, rewrite them, keep on building on this foundation. If your children are old enough you can include them in this process, and they can even write their own, which is amazing (be sure to keep copies of the versions your children make.) But don't sit down now and do this as a homeschooling project. Do your own for yourself first, remember the mom gets the oxygen mask first so she can better help her children. I suggest sharing your mission and vision statements with anyone closely involved in your homeschooling: your spouse, your parents, siblings, etc.

My Mission, My Vision

Your mission statement will explain your reason for homeschooling.

Your vision statement will describe how you envision doing this, especially with the future in sight. But remember, this is about you, not your children. *How you will manage homeschooling/your child's education.* Go ahead and be wordy, remember mine has been refined several times.

My current mission statement is:
I homeschool because I believe that the contemporary model of institutionalized learning is outdated and that I can provide a far superior education and lifestyle for my children myself.

My vision statement:
My vision is to foster my children's interests, encouraging them to deeply explore their activities and master skills they need to pursue their goals. I do

this by providing tools and resources for them, by positively encouraging them, by outsourcing any necessary aspects of their education, and by not overextending and burning myself out so that I may continue in this mode for all of my children for many years.

What is your mission and vision for yourself as a homeschooling parent?

Mission Statement

Vision Statement

CHAPTER TWO:
WHAT ARE YOU EVEN MODELING?

"Taking good care of yourself means the people in your life receive the best of you rather than what is left of you."

- Lucille Zimmerman

About a hundred or more times you've heard about putting your oxygen mask on before your child's, right? Or the expression "If mama ain't happy, ain't nobody happy"? If you are one of those rare versions of a mom who completely understood the need to take care of yourself from the day you first knew you were pregnant, then please skip this chapter, you have a workbench waiting for you and all those community center classes to attend. If you are one of those ordinary moms currently or frequently somewhere too close to burnout, then please read on.

Early in my homeschooling journey, during a Waldorf Parent-child course I took, I was told about the need to have my own hobbies and to take care of myself, how I would be modeling these behaviors to my children. I got that message twisted. At that point I didn't really have my own hobbies anymore. I still loved to thrift shop, but no longer to coordinate quirky creative outfits; rather I was on the hunt for clothes for my growing little guys. I also still loved to go for walks, but I no longer did this in urban areas where I liked to take photographs and see art along the way; instead I did most of my walking in the form of hiking in natural, green areas which I felt were safer for children and healthier, and when I did whip out my camera it focused on how cute they were and recording all their joys. In that parenting class we learned how to knit so that we could teach our children to knit to build their focus stamina and other good things like that. Knitting is an immensely relaxing hobby for many people, but I never quite got to that level as I was always knitting cute things for my kids. I never once knitted anything for myself. If you are thinking how great it was of me to be so selfless, stop it. I wasn't really being selfless, I needed to see some productivity in my work, some value to it. It wasn't selfless per se, just more busy work. And definitely not a hobby for me!

I've actually done this quite a bit during my adult life. For instance, after I left my job at our family business I was feeling a bit down that I didn't have any cute new things in quite awhile. No accessories, no cute new skirt or shoes- nothing, as it goes when you're in financial strains. So one afternoon I found myself strolling around Ebay, looking for some enticing new thing when I wound up in the wrong section, looking at jewelry supplies instead of finished jewelry, and I got the idea to make myself something.

That idea very quickly expanded into making somethings to sell, as in, I never made myself anything but bought supplies to start up a new business! This was not as hairbrained as it sounds. I did have loads of experience making jewelry in my teens, as well as a background in art and photography (very important for selling product). It was just the whole business thing that I needed to learn how to do. It turned out well. I made a small but helpful profit for my family and learned a lot about selling and marketing online. But there is an ongoing problem I see here. Instead of doing something purely for me, I only do things that add a tangible, specific sort of value to my family. I had lost my own identity and appreciation for myself.

So many women are this way that you may even be thinking along the lines I did, *What's wrong with that? Isn't it good to be selfless for your family?* Not to the point of martyrdom, which is what many women like myself are conditioned into doing.

When we give everything to our children and our families, what is the message that our children receive? When we are out of balance like that it follows that our children go to extremes as well. They may end up feeling guilty and resenting us for sacrificing so much, for giving more than they would ever ask for of us. Or they go to the other end and become spoiled, entitled people who take so much more from this world than they give.

Modeling is the best way for children to learn. Science has backed it up that "Do as I say, not as I do," is not only hypocritical but it simply doesn't work. How can we ask our children to learn so many new things and explore the world so thoroughly, when we are not doing that ourselves?

This is a twisted, confusing message we give them. Unfortunately, many of the women I know, especially the homeschooling mamas, fall into this habit until their suffering becomes too great. For me, this saw me putting on a lot of weight rather than enjoying physical activities the way I like to and eating sugar-filled junk in search of the energy boosts I craved. I also experienced several bouts of depression, which I think were brought on by my frustration with feeling stuck in roles and routines I did not want to be in. I finally had to put myself first when I saw I was at risk of not being able to care for my children as best I could due to my health and emotional conditions. Will you be able to carry on with your mission and vision if you don't care of yourself too?

Hobbies, Activities, Joys

What do you like to do? List a dozen activities.

_____

_____

_____

_____

_____

_____

_____

_____

_____

_____

_____

_____

What did you like to do before you had children? List a dozen activities.

What enjoyable activities can you do for now, with the resources and time you immediately have available? These can be small things, baby steps to get back in the habit of caring for yourself. List at least half a dozen things.

What activities would you like to prioritize to be doing in the near future? Dream big, you do great things for others and can do them for yourself too. List at least half a dozen things.

Now start doing them! And be sure to keep a record of all the wonderful things you do for yourself in Chapter _.

Self-Care

I have known many homeschooling moms over the decades, all with different needs and approaches to self-care. While there is a well-overused cliche of a mom desperate to spend a few moments alone in the bathroom, whether she's relieving herself or taking a bubblebath, there are those rare women on the other end of the spectrum who insist on larger clumps of alone time. Recently I talked to a woman who spends a few days a month alone. This sounded luxurious to me! There have been periods of time in her motheringhood when this was not possible, but she soon felt amiss and made these solitude chunks happen again. Being the only child of a single mom, solitude is a norm for me and I have desperately longed for it throughout my childbearing years, yet I allowed myself to succumb to the overwhelming myth that mothers should never want to be away from their children. There were just so many battles I could fight at once. I suffered for letting that one go.

Having had seven children, and mostly working from home for the last twenty years, I have had many struggles with getting quality alone time, as well as neglecting many other aspects of self-care. While I had wanted to work from home so that I could be closer to my children, I hadn't envisioned being constantly with my children and really just couldn't find any easy breaks. When I was told (by several people) that I was being unreasonable and moms shouldn't want to escape their kids, I felt the intended shame. The best I could do for myself was to guiltily abuse solo errand runs. Once or twice a month I would pop out "real quick" for just one thing, remaining gone for up to six hours. Six hours of time alone to myself once every two weeks or so - what a hedonist I had become!

When my family lived in a rural village in the High Atlas Mountains, after two years of being left alone to do all the caring for my children two or more weeks out of every month I finally had my breaking point, and insisted on my own vacations. My husband couldn't figure out a way to take a vacation with me let alone with the entire family, although he did get his break from all of us every month, whether he saw it that way or not. I could no longer accept this as just the way it was. It didn't make any sense that I was meant to live at this relentless pace. Some people truly think we moms are designed - by our Maker or evolution - to deal with the constant needs of our children and even our husbands.

I started taking 3-5 day vacations with just two of my kids at a time. For a mom of seven, two kids can feel like an immense break, especially the older ones who can do their own personal care. Now, I currently spend two weeks a year away from my family, fully rejuvenating myself, and I actively encourage other women to do so in my running retreats. Next year I will spend a month away from my family. Can you imagine an entire month? Probably not; you may likely be in that stage where you are struggling to spend more than fifteen seconds alone. I hate to be all "Do as I say, not as I..." but I truly hope that you can see your own value sooner than I did. I was at the point of being physically quite ill and questioning my sanity. There's a saying in Islam, 'You become the people you spend forty days with.' I was spending all my time with children. I didn't feel very articulate or refined at all!

My Steps to Optimizing Self-Care

You can do self-care in small steps, aiming for tiers of better and better self-care. And when I say "optimal" I don't mean lavish, I mean what a human body needs and deserves.

Right here, write a commitment to yourself to make ever increasing alone time to rejuvenate and become a better and better version of yourself, be it for you, your family, greater society or your Creator- we all appreciate you doing well for yourself. Perhaps in a freestyle way, write out how and where you can find tiny windows of time for yourself and how you can plan to increase them:

List a dozen things you would like to do solely for yourself:

List a dozen things you would really like to try:

List half a dozen places you would like to go within three hours of your home, but just never get to:

List half a dozen places in the world you would like to go:

Physical Well-Being

Hopefully this seems silly to you, but unfortunately many of us forget to do basic physical caring of our bodies while being immersed in caring for others. If you are regularly practising the basics (brushing your teeth and hair, showering, exfoliating, taking needed/wanted supplements, getting regular exercise) then use this chart to build on getting better basics: regular haircuts, wardrobe updates, counselling, or other therapeutic wellbeing services. Maybe you would benefit from visiting a nutritionist, massage therapist, reflexologist, or similar professional? You fill in the blanks with things you would like to do to optimally take care of yourself and use the following blank pages for your own customized tracking. For instance, I am currently detailed journaling my sleep habits in order to get better rest.

FULL BODY CHECK-IN

How Regularly Do You Want To Do This?	Tooth Brushing	A Skin Care Routine	Exercise	Visiting The ------------- ----
Daily				
Weekly				
Monthly				
Annually				

How Regularly Do You Want To Do This?				
Daily				
Weekly				
Monthly				
Annually				

TRACKING MY PATH TO BETTER AND BETTER WELL-BEING

Annuals and Proactivity

How are your teeth? How is your diet? If homeschooling doesn't affect your blood pressure, you may be a zombie. If you care so much about your kids that you homeschool them, then why wouldn't you take the best care of their best primary teacher? This check-in isn't meant to guilt you at all. We just get too busy and forget about or put ourselves off too often. When there are financial constraints involved, our health is often completely taken out of consideration. Let's find a way to get your body some of the tender love and care you can access. Personally, I have recently recognized that skin cancer is semi-common in my family and that I need to regularly wear sunblock, so first I bought some cheap junk while I kept an eye out for a sunscreen that is ideal for my skin and needs.

Specific Areas to Optimize Health	Current state, last check-up or other related service	What would you ideally like to have done here?	How can you plan to take care of this?
Annual Check-up, Any Special Concerns?			
How is The Blood Pressure?			
Cancer Screenings (What is common in your family?)			
Dental (You know gum disease can be passed to the kids?)			
Emotional Wellbeing (Be real honest with yourself here, mama)			
Mammogram and Pap-Smear			
Skin Cancer Check and Prevention			

Specific Areas to Optimize Health	Current state, last check-up or other related service	What would you ideally like to have done here?	How can you plan to take care of this?

What logistics do you need to get yourself to check ups, dental appointments, and other health care priorities? Childcare, transport, money, etc.

Who can you ask for help and exactly what help can you ask them for?

Soulful Emotional Check-in

Whatever your path, there is a meditation, prayer, self-reflection practice that guides your body to connect to your soul. As a Muslim I am scheduled to formally pray five times a day, but sometimes - stressful times especially - I find my concentration completely gone and I just physically go through the motions of prayer without making any real connection. Developing the *kushu* to have this concentration is essentially a form of meditation. I didn't realize this for years as I was too busy trying to develop my kushu to learn other forms of meditation! Fortunately I happened to attend an event that included a guided visualization exercise and I loved it.

Having a professional guide me through the exercise, imagining the story and setting she described, and then facilitated discussion afterwards was ideal. It had a lasting effect on me, raising my awareness of certain aspects of my personality. I was inspired to try more and found Neuro-linguistic programming (NLP) one of the few forms of therapy readily available to me locally. NLP has also benefited me to further shift my mindset. Really I wouldn't mind doing these things very regularly, but that homeschooling mom lifestyle... so I am also slowly working my way through the numerous styles of meditation and self-reflection exercises available on Youtube videos. This has been a great way to sample from the scope of practices on my own time and, of course, for free. I also continue to build on my Islamic practices of emotionally centering devotionals, such as dhikr-reciting affirmative phrases, and I am planning to attend a soulful retreat this year.

How much time in your week do you think you deserve to nurture your soul? Be generous with yourself!

How much time in a day do you deserve to nurture your soul? If you aren't already, take small steps to get there.

What are some forms of meditation you would like to explore? Where will you start?

"Self-care is never a selfish act - it is simply good stewardship of the only gift I have, the gift I was put on earth to offer others. Anytime we can listen to true self and give the care it requires, we do it not only for ourselves, but for the many others whose lives we touch."

- Parker J. Palmer

CHAPTER THREE:

THIS IS HOW AWESOME YOU ARE AS MEASURED BY THE GREAT THINGS YOUR OFFSPRING DID

I am finally at a point where I can easily shrug off anyone's suggestion that I put my children in school. I usually even have to stifle a giggle over how ridiculous and presumptuous people are being. Last week I had coffee with one of my son's tutors while we waited for this perpetually late son. The sweet tutor started to question me about my children not being in school, how were they going to learn anything? Instead of going on a long-winded explanation I realised that this man didn't even recognize his own role in my child's education. I simply told him, "Zak and my other kids have other tutors like you, they are learning everything." He seemed to ponder my response for just a moment and then the conversation easily redirected. Thank God it was as simple as that, as you know it often isn't!

Getting to this point took me years. Unfortunately I used to take everyone's advice and 'concern' to heart. *Surely they are worried about my children and want what is best for them, perhaps I am doing my children a grave disservice!* No. These conversations are almost always occurring because the person knows absolutely nothing about homeschooling, even if they think they do) and is having a gut reaction to it based fully in fear. *What if their entire educational experience was wrong? What if they could have done something different for 12+ years of their life? What if education can really be laidback and fun?* Few of these people even get to the point in the conversation where they can learn that homeschooling can be laidback and fun because they are purely reactionary and freaking out on you.

Beyond a couple of initial, assumptious questions, most people never put an effort into really understanding the process and empathizing with your choice. They essentially just attack you. Don't take that to heart! It's only about you in that you are a sort of conduit presenting that very frightening reality to them - there *is* a different way to spend those 12+ years. It's not your fault they didn't know that before and it's not your fault they are scared to fully consider it for their own family. But whatever initiates your moments of self doubt, here is where you can build a list, privately gloating all of your children's, and in turn your accomplishments.

I know what this looks like, but it's really not about the children here. Of course it's wonderful to have these records for when all is said and done (your children will love having this) but this is a list to keep you going. In those moments of self doubt you can return to this list and nod along, recognizing that you are a big part of creating capable cool little people. This list is your own self-made pep talk.

Create these lists for each child. Our children simultaneously go through wildly different life stages and it's a real strain to sway back and forth between them, but kudos to you for doing it! It is difficult to maintain balance. Keeping these lists may help you to see when you leaning too far one way or another (frankly giving one child too much attention over another), but the overall goal is to have pile of booty here that will lift you when you are feeling discouraged or like you are failing. I've started off some possible sections for you, I'm sure you will think of loads once you get going.

Physical Accomplishments

Kindness/Empathy Deeds

Academic Achievements

Challenges Attempted

Creative Efforts

"Parents can only give good advice or put them on the right paths, but the final forming of a person's character lies in their own hands."

-Anne Frank

CHAPTER FOUR:
THE GREAT THINGS I DID

Here is your list! Okay, actually the kids will really benefit from this too. Even if they never see this list, they will see most of the great things you do- the things you model and inspire them to do more of and better. This list will be like building a staircase, encouraging you to go higher and higher.

I work in media-making and feel like my life is an open book (see Part Two), but often forget to share these vignettes of my life with my children. While I keep this list for myself, I also regularly go through my phone's photo gallery with my children. Ultimately I would like to get a projector so I can occasionally do this as a family affair, harkening back to that golden age of gathering around for family home movies and slideshows from holidays abroad. While mainstream movies and shows have long made fun of these gatherings and especially the people (and by people I mean men) who recorded and shared these moments, in my experience my children love to see what we have been doing as a family and as individuals. This generation regularly shares images and their daily doings with their peers while perhaps shutting out their family. Perhaps this is a generational discord, as we are more weary of overuse of social media and the internet in general, though among homeschoolers it is often natural for young people to share with their family, the core of their life. While the kids may have timelines and archives to review many of their activities and accomplishments, do you?

This list is your personal history. It will allow you to see how much you truly have done in your life. Reviewing it resets your trajectory. Be lavish with making this list, it's the ultimate feel good seeing how good you really are! I initially try to make my list in a chronological order, but now it's just an immense mosaic and wonderfulness.

List everything you have ever done that you feel good about:

"Children have never been very good at listening to their elders, but they have never failed to imitate them."

-James Baldwin

CHAPTER FIVE:
NEVER WILL I EVER AGAIN

I often feel like I am slow to learn things. I'll read about something, a theory or whatever, but not really get it until long after I experience it in person. Sometimes I have to experience the same things over and over again, even painful things. For instance I seldom recognise when someone is being jealous of me. That's a hard thing to pinpoint, isn't it? But it happens, and people act, well, bitchy towards me, and I think I that *I must have done som...* oh yeah, they are jealous.

It's wonderful when I am able to see patterns, set boundaries and otherwise change things I don't like for myself or my children. Still, I'm not a stickler for try anything once. What if I was having an off day the first time? Maybe I should give it another try. However long or many tries it takes me to figure it out, there are some things I just won't do again. Still I usually have to remind myself what the reasons are that I shouldn't. For instance, when going on outings with many other children I won't stay longer than three hours. After three hours at least one of my kids starts falling apart and I am fairly tired, but still need to get them home and do plenty of work with them when I get there. If I stay any longer I will be fully exhausted and plenty unpleasant when we do finally get home and I still have to do loads of mothering. I've had to learn this lesson the hard way. It doesn't matter how much I paid for the thing we are doing, how much I adore other parents at the event, how much fun we all are having - if I don't make an exit at the three-hour mark there will be ugly consequences.

Your time as a homeschooling parent is extra precious. You don't get that Monday through Friday break that other moms usually get, so it's best to be protective of your energy reserves. There are going to be experiences, activities, maybe curriculum, or even people you don't want to deal with again if you can avoid it, even when people nag at you to "Just give it a try" or "Just this once". Nope, know your limits. Make reminders for yourself here. Go ahead and rant if it makes you feel better, it will help you remember exactly why you'll never ever again.

Never Will I Ever Again...

CHAPTER SIX:
THE VERY BAD DAY ARSENAL

I hope this chapter is rarely useful to you. Being proactive and pre-planning self-care right into your daily and long-term scheduling is ideal, but some days just suck, so let's prepare for those here with a list of things you can do to take a cheat day or break from the kids without fully getting away. As you notice activities your children really enjoy and can mostly do on their own, note them here so you can use them on days you really need them. Stashing items away is what I find works best. Or this may just be extra screen time. Don't feel bad about that! Maybe list a few shows that are edutainment just to feel better about your attempt to stay homeschooley. I've included a few that work well for me.

Toddler

Surprise box: Fill a box or purse with random yet interesting items from around the house then give it to your toddler to go through and play with.

Silly Putty can be less of a hassle than clay or dough if your child is old enough for it, stow some away for a bad day.

Primary School Aged

Tuck away an enticing book series or game they have been wanting, pull it out when you need some down time.

Dazzling art sets, such as markers or mixed medium sets with their own cases are often good for a few hours of quiet time.

Tweens

Personalized journal/art book: Stash away blank journals and stickers when they are on sale or you find cool ones.

"The struggles we endure today will be the 'good old days' we laugh about tomorrow."

- Aaron Lauritsen

(Please God, let it be true!)

PART TWO:
My Mostly Abridged Homeschooling Memoir

"You are limitless in thought. Your mind is a treasure. You have infinite potential. Realize your gift. Realize that you yourself are the gift."

- Akiroq Brost

CHAPTER SEVEN:
HOMESCHOOLING MYSELF

I've unwittingly made a lot of unpopular choices during my life. Not at all bad choices, just unusual and easily (mis)judged. As a teen I was drawn to the poetic lyrics and moody rhythms of alternative music, and the dark, almost hidden theatrics of goth and punk clothes. I went to art school instead of choosing a more profitable profession for my studies. I picked a grossly misunderstood and/or little known at that time religion for the foundation of my lifestyle. I married someone from another culture, from another country. Incidentally he was also the only person in his family to make such an unorthodox choice. I also moved overseas to my husband's home country, which gives me the odd misnomer "expat" even though I understood it to be one of my US-born privileges to freely move about this world. I homebirthed most of my babies, and I've had way more children than the national average in most countries. I make other personal and medical choices that some people spend a good chunk of their lives battling against. None of these things were done to piss anyone else off, though sometimes I have been accused of that. Rather, they were done for my personal aesthetics, ethics, or because my gut drove me to do them. But the one thing that has had the most external and internal combativeness has been my decision to homeschool my children.

Unlike many of my life choices, homeschooling was something that had percolated in me for decades. After just a couple of months in high school, I left that environment at only fifteen years old. I knew that I wasn't going to make it nearly three years in that setting. I had been in the school system for ten years and it looked like exactly more of the same would be happening over the next three years. My situation there wasn't at all unique. Think of all the kids who sat in classrooms ten to twelve years, only to drop out in those final couple of years. Yet I wasn't choosing to be a drop out. I didn't feel like I was done with my formal education, but I was ready for something markedly different. I wanted to go to the local community college where I saw my friends dropping in and out of classes that sparked their interests. This made perfect sense to me. Why shouldn't we be able to explore our interests without years of commitment? This was the age when we were supposed to be discovering who we are. I knew there had to be a way to get to higher education sooner. I also vaguely knew that a neighbor of mine was a teacher doing something different with continued education for high school students and that there were kids who got help to leave school early due to family, personal, or other crisis-like situations. I didn't feel that I was fully in crisis, but suspected that he could help me.

He advised me on how to enroll in a program that was set up for at-risk students who were facing dropping out of or being kicked out of school. Once a week I went onto the campus to drop off a week's worth of school work and pick up the next week's work. If I needed any help on a subject, my once-a-week teacher could help me on it, otherwise I was on my own, spending most of my time at the library, watching films, or making art. As part of my course work I also enrolled in German (foreign language) and tennis (physical education) at the local community college I had been pining for. The plan was that I do this for one semester, until I was a second semester tenth grader or sixteen years old, the requirements then to take the GED (General Education Development exam and receive the equivalent of a high school diploma). I would then be done with my "lower" education. This system was formally called "Home Ed." I passed the test and began attending community college full time at sixteen years old. College cost much less almost three decades ago, so I easily took whatever subjects piqued my interest while gathering a pile of credits to transfer to a four-year university. This time felt like what high school was supposed to feel like - happy, engaging, explorative, freer.

It wasn't until after I began homeschooling my own children that I recognized that I had chosen homeschooling for myself too, although technically I had unschooled myself. But long before I walked off campus at fifteen years old, I had an interest in homeschooling, though I didn't make the connection on that day or even two decades later when I frighteningly decided to homeschool my first son. In the afternoons of my primary school years I was a precocious fan of the daytime talk shows that came on after Gilligan's Island and Scooby Doo. I would switch away from Thundercats and Transformers to watch Phil Donahue and young Oprah Winfrey. I didn't understand a lot of what they talked about, but loved the enthusiasm and thoughtfulness they gave to all topics. One rare topic I did understand and happened to catch on at least two occasions was families who choose to keep their children out of school, the parents educating the kids at home.

This was in the 1980s, and these kids, like a few still today, were presented as prodigies with unique talents and intelligence, who without the constrictions of school were able to excel. This didn't strike me as a chicken or egg scenario, it was obvious to me that if we didn't waste so much time at the mundanities in school we could more thoroughly explore and improve on our personal passions. As someone who enjoyed reading and researching since a young age (I'm one of those kids who read the encyclopedia and who often spent school lunch period in the library) it wasn't lost on me that "my schooling was getting in the way of my education," as Mark Twain famously said. I was much happier to take my education into my own hands, to more freely and deeply explore my own interests. Still, that wasn't my immediate intention when, almost hastily, I decided to homeschool my first son.

CHAPTER EIGHT:
THE GUINEA PIG CHILD

Throughout my first pregnancy I felt desperate to find a way to work from home after he was born. Whining to all of my friends and acquaintances about this (known linguistically as "networking"), had worked well for me. When my son was just a few weeks old I began doing public relations freelancing under the tutelage of a friend. I knew nothing about the field but was enthusiastic and hardworking, grateful to be doing what is often suggested - "Work from home!" - but is not at all easy to find or build. In these couple of years prior to 9/11, before the economy tanked, this work was the most lucrative I had ever had. We lived a comfortable middle-class lifestyle with a touch of hippy carefreeness.

When my first two children were very young, our rented wood-floored, real brick-exterior duplex was on a dogwood tree lined neighborhood in Portland, Oregon, a cinematic-friendly area where many movies are filmed. It was idyllic-looking, but let me tell you it was the whitest place I have ever lived. And since, as you may know, my children are not white, it wasn't as ideal as it may sound. Even while we lived there, having moved from Brooklyn in search of more "space," I was still pining for a backyard my children would be able to freely do that outdoor yard stuff kids do. While I worked in the second bedroom makeshift home office upstairs in the early mornings, my husband started the day with the boys. By the time I was done he had either made, or at least started on, a multi-dish lunch. My husband was a chef when we met while I was a baker. Either before or after lunch I would take my eldest, Badier, (and either my pregnant belly or newborn) to one of the many lush local parks in Portland where he could play on the equipment with abandon and explore the woods for treasures and critters to watch. He would snack on string cheese, rice cakes, and other wholesome goodies bought at the food co-op where I volunteered in exchange for a little discount. We had a weekly delivery of an organic seasonal-produce box to our door, while I waited for a coveted spot to open up at the local community garden. I never got my spot before we moved, but I did keep a small container-garden on our balcony. I continue to container garden today while still dreaming of finding myself a plot somewhere. Back then (and now fifteen years later) the central focus in our living room was a cubby unit filled with engaging, educational toys, books, and activity items. When Badier was about three years old I transitioned to more open-ended, "natural" style toys made of wood and wool instead of plastic. This was before the mainstream backlash and restrictions against dangerous BPA content in children's plastic toys, but I had caught wind of the then conspiracy about it. I took parenting very seriously, as we do, and wanted my children to have a true childhood full of play, beauty and wonder.

One afternoon I was in the kitchen when a neighbor, who was a ridiculously busy working mama, came to my back door for a rare visit. We stood at the white tiled counter exchanging pleasantries, and then she told me the reason for her call. It was time to pre-register for kindergarten at the local elementary school. My son was only three years old, so I hadn't thought about kindergarten at all. She suspected as much and was letting me know now as the school was the best in the district and much sought after. Many people outside of the neighborhood illegally used friends' and family members' addresses to enroll their children there, and there was a lengthy waiting list that I "should" get on immediately. I can't remember another time in my life that I felt this way, but you know that overused saying "hit with a ton of bricks"? That's how I felt. Like the ceiling had opened up and the enormous yellow claw of a Caterpillar dumped a ton of grey cement cedar blocks on me. My well-crafted world felt like it was bottoming out.

I thought, How am I going to do this? Here I've been doing the best for my kids, feeding them organic healthy foods, giving them the best developmental toys, practicing conscious parenting, homebirthing, extended breastfeeding, cloth diapering... and now I have to hand my son over to an absolute stranger for the majority of his waking hours?! While institutionalized schooling is pretty standard stuff in our society, it still felt like it crept up on me. It didn't feel right at all. After my neighbor left and I stood in the kitchen trying to repel rather than absorb this shock, one word popped into the tidal pool that my cerebral matter was becoming: homeschool. Oh my God, it was a like an aftershock I hadn't braced for. How would I do that!?

Looking back, it is quite amazing that I wasn't able to see any of the connections. Homeschooling, although an absolute norm just two generations ago and something I had even done myself, was that far removed from my conscious. Being in the hotbed of young progressive and liberal families with religious evangelicalism on the outskirts, I was in the prime location to learn everything I needed to know about homeschooling.

Not only did our Multnomah County library system carry at least a dozen books on homeschooling, they also delivered them right to my door as soon as it got to my turn on the waiting list. I read all of the major works and theories available to me on homeschooling: John Taylor Gatto, Maria Montessori, Waldorf and unschooling theories, and general how-to's. Waldorf pedagogy was the one that gelled best with me. It was both arty and woodsy, gentle and deep, with high percentages of its followers attending university which was an opportunity I was concerned about my child having access to without attending conventional schooling. I learned that a full-sized Waldorf school recently opened in the city and they had many courses for parents. Another thing I liked about the general Waldorf community is that they encourage parents to continue their own personal growth and education. I immediately began attending a "Parent and Child" course to immerse myself in the style.

My son and I both loved the bi-weekly classes. We sat side by side at the round wooden table with legs cut perfectly to a preschooler's height, rolling out prepped sourdough, and then imbibing its baking aromas while singing songs and learning stories that always included hand and body gestures. At snack time we sipped lightly sweetened chamomile tea, and Badier let the other attendees know that he preferred temari over soy sauce for his brown rice. The mothers (which all the adults were, even though it was for "parents") exchanged info on where to buy organic wool, cotton, and silk clothing for children. My bubble rolled and expanded, my idyllic mothering days continued. I had gathered my curriculum, supplies, and support network. I was ready to begin homeschooling.

Badier was about four years old when we started homeschooling in the Waldorf style, with tiny puppets and storytelling to teach math, and essentially coloring to learn the alphabet. My son had liked to be read to since infancy, but didn't actually do much pretend play that involved creating his own fantastical scenarios. Even when playing with other children he was more inclined to lead with large movements - running and building - than following any elaborate storylines. And while he did like to paint, I hadn't noticed before that he didn't care to use crayons. I bought those age-appropriate fat crayons, better for a short, chubby fingered grasp and later beeswax blocks, but when he did draw he instinctively reached for pens, not even pencils, like the adults around him used, of course. But drawing was still very rare; he liked to do bigger, more full body things. He was the first born and hadn't been in daycare or had those things modeled to him, so I figured he would just need time to settle into these new activities. Nope. Much later I would learn he is a classic Kinesthetic learner, but in those early days there was only so much new information I could acquire. Our parent-to-teacher and child-to-student transitions weren't flowing as I hoped. It felt forced to me, as if I was playing a role I didn't want to take on and it seemed to feel forced to him too. He just wasn't interested in playing school. I was frustrated. But as always, determined. I hit the books again.

CHAPTER NINE:
UPDATING MY STYLE ALREADY?

Unschooling was a method I had skimmed over in my initial homeschool readings because it sounded implausible to me. You do nothing and your kid gets smart? It didn't make sense. This was because I hadn't deschooled myself. I didn't even discover deschooling until some years later and still feel that I need to return to it almost seasonally, annually peeling off the layers of indoctrination that occured in my 10+ years of formal education. Relooking at unschooling I found it to be true that my child could, and already did, learn without my directly teaching him. Without constant diligence to teach him things prior to beginning homeschooling, my son had managed to learn plenty of things. He did have an innate curiosity that led him to explore and research various interests. When I was open to playing along and fostering those moments, we both learned loads. I am now a hobbyist entomologist, and due to my second son being ridiculously well-versed in the types and functions of rocket fuel, well I know a lot about that too. There is contemporary support for "knowing a little about a lot" being handier than just being an expert in one highly specific thing. For first-hand experience I can say that this is one of the many benefits of homeschooling; we the parents can learn a lot of fun, interesting things at our children's elbows. I began to think child-led learning could be plausible, except for certain subjects like math and reading. This is a common, tentative approach to beginning unschooling.

In addition to plotting math-teaching moments, I pushed on with teaching my son to read. Formal lessons in reading remained a struggle, but I saw improvements in the rest of our teacher-parent-student-child relationship. Wherever he toed a door, I offered to swing it open for him. I gave him ample room - as in most of the house! - and resources to pursue his interests. Building was a big one and I had to purchase duct tape almost daily. A hardware co-op certainly would have been handy. My son was happy, energetic, precocious, and seemingly pretty smart. I felt good about how our homeschooling was progressing.

CHAPTER TEN:
THE PARTNER PARENT

During these initial stages of learning about and beginning homeschooling my husband was very supportive. Sort of. I studied up fastidiously on everything homeschooling and regurgitated the high and most interesting notes to him: that educating at home could be done, that it was almost always better than institutionalized learning, that I had all the "qualifications" or rather looked the part of an ideal candidate for a homeschooling mom, that most homeschoolers excelled and went on to higher education, that it was an exciting lifestyle and so on. Looking back, I see that his nodding along wasn't as supportive as a co-parent can be, though it was his best. Maybe he didn't fully understand or believe what I was proposing, maybe he wasn't as forthcoming as he could have been - wires were definitely crossed, though if there were red flags, I ignored them.

I fully admitted that I did not want to relive the advanced math years with our children and either my husband would have to do it or we would use tutors. In our children's early years I often pushed their father to teach them some of the other four languages he knows, but that was never followed through on. I have had many people ask me why my kids aren't naturally bilingual or why their father doesn't teach them other languages. We adults should understand that you can't force other people to do things they don't want to. And not everyone will directly tell you "no" that they aren't going to do something they don't want to do. Looking back I believe that I expected him to actively participate in our homeschooling endeavors, just as he did participate greatly on our domestic front. Still, like most people I was/am conditioned to take on the brunt of household affairs as I am the woman in the relationship, and homeschooling neatly fell into my domestic affairs. I took our sons to all their activities - the parent-child course, art workshops, gymnastics,and nearly all of their social outings. Occasionally we went on hikes as a family. We frequently ate out as a family, though that habit died down with the more and more children we had. The great bulk of homeschooling fell onto my shoulders. This wasn't too noticeable to me when we had two small children and a lot of flexibility in our work schedules, but those dynamics all changed in the next few years.

CHAPTER ELEVEN:
NOW FOR SOME THINGS VERY DIFFERENT

When the economy bottomed out after 9/11 we decided it was a good time to move to Morocco. Before we married we had agreed to live in (not just visit) my husband's home country at some point, though like many things we had never discussed any details. I knew little to nothing about the culture, and although I had met many of my husband's Moroccan friends, I hadn't met any of his family until his dad came to visit just before our move overseas. Admittedly, when we married I only knew where Morocco was because an old roommate had gone on one date with a Moroccan guy and we looked it up on a map when she got home. I hadn't been overseas myself for longer than a few days, still I didn't fear it. I was happy to be part of a multi-cultural family and again hit the books looking to get any vague grasp on cultural faux pas and to have somewhat of an idea of what to expect. I even took a couple semesters of French at Portland Community College as Arabic wasn't available at that time.

While I am shocked to regularly meet foreign people living in Morocco who are grossly ignorant of the most basic of Muslim or Moroccan ways, there is also a danger in relying on many of the guidebooks and blogs which often don't know what they are talking about, mistaking inference for fact and pushing their own biases. This is one of the many beauties of the privilege of moving beyond your physical and cultural borders: nothing is at it seems. Every day in Morocco, just as every day at homeschooling, I have the opportunity to learn myself and this life anew.

That said, moving overseas is difficult whichever direction you go. People who have relocated say that the things you worry about beforehand won't matter once you are there, but there will be unforeseeable challenges which will certainly rattle your cage. It's a luxury to be able to pace yourself into the new territory as I did since I didn't have to work any more. The things I worried about most were communicating, as Morocco is a French, Arabic, Darija and Tshilhit speaking country whereas I had studied English, German, and Spanish in high school and college. Hastily taking French 1 and 2 gave me the littlest, but still an edge out of that anxiety of complete lack of communication skills. My pronunciation is still horrible sixteen years later, but it's proven occasionally helpful. What is even more helpful is that so many people here do speak some English. I have long given up on starting conversations in French or Darija, now I first test if my new acquaintance will work with me in a little Darenglish. My communication with my in-laws is still very limited though. I had also worried about cultural clashes with my in-laws and that I would offend them, as I regularly do people of my own culture so I guess I could have just accepted that would happen rather than worry about it. Something I didn't anticipate at all before our move was that my husband would randomly announce one day that we should register our four year old in school.

My commitment to homeschooling didn't waiver with the relocation. I had even collected loads of supplies I anticipated needing in Morocco, such as the Waldorfy art supplies I love, early reading books, and plenty of open-ended, pretend play toys- those things currently in our cubbies and baskets, still being used by my youngest children fifteen years later. In that first year here, however, my husband had a change of heart. Whether his commitment had always been weak, external pressures broke him, or perhaps he just thought our son would adjust better to the culture - I don't know, but I wasn't interested in any arguments. I had done all my legwork and was ready to settle in as a "homeschooler abroad" just like the few I had found online. At that time it was mostly foreign government employees or missionaries who were choosing to homeschool rather than subject their children to the strains of immersion in such a different culture or, of course, to keep them from being influenced by cultures and religions so potentially contradictory from their own. Frankly, these were not people I would want to be in a community with, but I found solace in knowing that what I was setting out to do was feasible. The husband and I argued about his decision for a week or so before I agreed to go see the schools.

"No such thing as the right time, situation or place. You have all it takes. Just dig within. Exhume all the greatness inside of you and transform the world with an inexhaustible drive and without fear of limitations."

- Chinonye J. Chidolue

CHAPTER TWELVE:
NOT ONE FOOT IN THE DOOR

The first school we visited, "a good school," was within a few blocks of our home. An intense sting of disinfectant was the first thing I noticed when we walked into the cool, as in low temperature, building. I suppose the aroma was meant to reassure parents. It was an old colonial period house - spacious rooms built around a staircase leading up to more but smaller rooms, all painted in institutional tones of blue and yellow that ultimately didn't add any warmth to the building. There wasn't any outdoor play place under the magnificent Mediterranean sky. The pedagogy and activities were what I would come to find out were pretty typical for this setting: singing along to cassette tapes, coloring (within the lines), and practicing letter and numeral writing. The equipment was lackluster, the teachers all wore clinical white smock-like coats and my son hid from them behind me during the brief tour. The only thing the school could offer that I couldn't do at home was language acquisition, which my husband could offer, and of course my son was picking up his grandparents' Tshilhit, even though his auntie spoke to him entirely in English. I had much fancier educational materials at home. And I knew from other mothers' experiences that it would very likely be quite upsetting to enter my child into a school where he did not speak the language of everyone else in it. Their children struggled through long painful periods that were simply accepted as par for the course. While it is now commonplace to find a few Anglophones in nearly any school setting here in Morocco, none of the children or teachers spoke English at this school. Why would I throw my child into this environment? This school was easy to reject.

The next school was just around the corner from this first one. Casablanca is an enormous city of 3.36 million people with several schools, both private and public, competing in every neighborhood. This school boasted an outdoor play area. The teacher walked me over to the window, pointing to a wide gated driveway with a couple of abandoned tricycles in it. "But we don't use it very often," she said. She downplayed all the playing aspects of their program, focusing on their academic activities. Parents didn't pay to send their children to school to play. With public universities being free in Morocco, the pressure to get into the best ones starts in preschool for better-heeled Moroccans who can afford to pay for privatized preschools. This was completely counter to the philosophy I was following of "better late than early." While I was laying out my reasons for rejecting this and any school, my husband was walking us towards another one. Again the headmaster seemed thrilled to have a potential "Nus-Nus" student: half Moroccan and half European (or even rarer half American). This school was several stories high, with the airy (read "empty of anything interesting or engaging") classrooms wrapped around an open courtyard. Again we were enthusiastically informed of their thorough and rigid course work - for four-year-olds. As we got to the portion of the interview where I would ask about their play program the students were being let out for a sort of recess period.

The headmaster walked over to a railing where we could observe the children playing in the courtyard, which was a simple cemented square, large enough to park maybe twenty small cars, absent of any play equipment. Like fish in a too-small aquarium, most of the kids were jogging or running around in a circle the circumference of the yard. Slower kids were chatting among themselves and larger kids were darting in and out of the packs from inner and outer circles. It was a slightly orchestrated chaos. There didn't seem to be any adult encouraging or directing them to do this groupish activity, there simply wasn't anything else to do! A lone ball lay off to one side, probably not being played with because I could only imagine the fights caused by one ball among nearly hundred kids. This was "the best school" within walking distance of our house. This school was worse than anything I could have imagined in the states, and that was where I had decided to opt out of institutionalized learning. I couldn't begin to understand what my husband was thinking, and he certainly didn't communicate his side well enough to be convincing to me otherwise. I was relieved that our options proved unacceptable. We dropped the issue. Or so I thought.

Within a few weeks I would learn that Lhassan had kept looking for schools in that traditional Moroccan networking way, asking everyone he knew what was the best school they knew. I was doing my own networking online, but only gathering more assurance against schooling based on people's frustrating and even frightful experiences. Though it is illegal, corporal punishment still happens in classrooms. Even when children don't experience it on their own body, nearly all are subjected at some point to witnessing other students being abused. And of course the strong academic drive so many people lauded only pushed me further and further away. In his searches, I'm not sure how many schools Lhassan went and saw on his own, but he finally found one about a forty-minute drive from our house that he thought I should see. It was a private religious school. They had a lawn with a slide on it. My husband was convinced it was a great school. I reasoned with myself that surely he wouldn't look beyond a forty-minute drive! I would go see this one just to get him off my back once and for all.

CHAPTER THIRTEEN:
A HOMESCHOOLING MOM AND A SCHOOLING DAD?

Another headteacher, this time wearing a Muslim man's long plain gown - a thobe - enthusiastically gave me the rundown of the school. Our son would be learning all the regular subjects - Arabic, Math, Reading (in Arabic), plus Quran - they also taught English as a second language, to children as young as three he said, but still the main instruction was done in a foreign-to-my son language. And from what I know of our religion, children shouldn't be formally taught Quran until they are seven years old, before they we are directed to "let them play." There is also newer Western research indicating that children learn important skills, such as social relations, motor skills, and more through open play and shouldn't be formally educated until around seven years old. Why is everyone so eager to make sweet little kids into studious pupils? But maybe the typical academic schedule wasn't the worst thing about the school.

The program was all day, with a break for lunch that some of the children went home to eat and others stayed at the school to eat. If we enrolled our son, our options were to drive back and forth for a total of an hour and a half through stressful urban traffic four times a day or only twice a day, and leave our four year old child at school from nine o'clock in the morning to five o'clock in the evening. Why was this getting worse instead of better? I refused to talk about this school, or any school, with my husband anymore.

My husband pressed on, convinced this school was the best option for our child. When he brought it up I would silently seethe, envisioning my son gone most of his waking hours, surrounded by strangers, most of whom he couldn't even communicate with. I imagined myself doing all the labor of getting him ready, but the horrendous commuting was too over the top for me. Daily driving in traffic is noted as one of the best ways to completely stress our bodies out; why would I choose that? I could not envision myself doing it. My parents had commuted throughout my childhood, the distance expanding as I got older. I absolutely resented all that time wasted, as I saw it, and had sworn I would never do it myself. While some people make good use of the drive time with their children, he wouldn't be with me for more than half those hours I returned home or to get him. Instead I would be white-knuckling it through traffic, angry at myself for going against every nerve in my body. The closest I came to agreeing to put our son in this (or any school) was telling my husband if that was what he wanted he could do it all himself.

I wasn't bluffing when I said that I would have nothing to do with helping getting my son ready for and transporting him to and from school. I wouldn't buy the school clothes, keep them laundered (and for my husband's preference that would include ironing), wake our son every morning (oh I forgot to mention, kids in Morocco go to school six days a week), get him ready, make his breakfast, make his lunch, and drive him back and forth. I didn't expect my husband to accept this workload which he so readily chose for me. Fortunately he didn't, and my son was not enrolled in school. Enrolling him in school was completely taken out of our discussions.

CHAPTER FOURTEEN:
HOMESTAYING

After the nearly-schooled hurdle was passed, our first few months in Morocco were fairly idyllic. We intended to live in my in-laws' home only initially, but carried on there as our immediate future was so uncertain. Would my husband work in the family business? Would he have to start his own business? Would I have to get a job? While the circumstances were stressful for us, still my sons benefited from that quality multi-generational time with their grandparents and auntie. I struggled to get our outings anywhere near the level of abundance that Parks and Recreations had provided in the US, but young children are easy enough to entertain. We did plenty of water and messy play on the balcony, explored the greenery of a public garden space a little more than locals might ("Stay off the grass!" signs were common), and found a great park a short taxi ride from the house. After several months it became clear that my husband's work opportunities would not be at the level we needed to thrive in Morocco in our usual middle-class lifestyle. When I became pregnant we repeated a search initiative similar to our school hunting experience, this time for a desirable birthing option.

My second son had been comfortably born at home and I was hooked on homebirthing. I hoped to do the same with my third. This was a near impossibility in urban Morocco where everyone now births in hospitals and clinics, most without their partner by their side. While my medical preferences have clashed with the mainstream medical field in the USA, I am usually able to find comfortable alternatives, such as naturopathic doctors, delayed vaccination schedule, and so on. I wasn't easily finding anything like that in Morocco. It exists, but is so few and far between, and this was in the days before 3G and having steady home internet. The further along I got in my pregnancy, the more I was ready to go home.

Except, I didn't have a home in the US anymore; we had packed everything into a half-sized container and shipped it by vessel to Casablanca. Two rooms of my in-laws' house were stuffed floor to ceiling with my stretch wrap-covered furniture and dozens of meticulously labeled boxes of household things. My husband also needed to return to the US as part of his visa status. We had to quickly figure out what we were going to do. My mom offered for us to live with her for awhile in her new home state of Alaska. I hadn't yet been to Alaska. She had been pining to visit or live there for many years before finally doing so. Raised in California, I wasn't wild about snow, which is on the ground in Alaska from about October to May, but I also didn't want to establish an entire new household as we hoped to return to Morocco revitalized and better ready to start a life there. My husband, my two young boys and my just barely still-legal-to-fly self flew to Alaska, with wooden animal figurines and our favourite picture books maximizing our luggage allowance.

CHAPTER FIFTEEN:
REPATRIATING IS COMPLICATED

Alaska was weird. I was weird. Another thing I didn't know about moving overseas is that things are also challenging when you return to your homeland. Apparently you may have changed significantly, but home has not. I was thrilled to return to so many comforts and conveniences, I was grumpy to return to the same old ignorances and biases. And I wasn't simply moving back in. Let alone the same house, my mother and I had not lived in the same state for over a decade. Initially it was wonderful to have my mommy, but the relationship became strained quickly. We are both strong-willed, and neither of us was used to acting like family in close quarters. My own growing little family needed to live elsewhere though my husband and I were not financially prepared for that as we had invested our money into a small business. I was completely unfamiliar with social services and later found out that we had been eligible for several helpful services. Instead we struggled alone through the most financially difficult period of my life. I remember standing in an aisle at the grocery store having to choose between milk for my children or pain reliever for me. Thank God it wasn't pain reliever for them because you know what I ultimately chose. That kind of poverty, with three children in tow, is something I wouldn't wish on anyone. But there was one area where we lucked out, and that greatly improved things for us.

Alaska is probably the best state to homeschool in. I hadn't known about this for our first several months living there. I continued homeschooling on my own, using the library, and other materials I had, until an acquaintance filled me in on this fact. Alaska has a sort of homeschooling school district that allows families to choose from multiple homeschooling situations, such as online and distance schooling, or the do-it-yourself style of choosing curriculums that are paid for through a homeschool allotment. Receiving a homeschool allotment meant accessing more and better materials for my children. We even received a computer from the school district. Of course some people find this shocking - to essentially receive money or be subsidized to homeschool - but considering that each school receives tens of thousands of dollars for each pupil that attends, why should families who chose to homeschool be burdened with all the costs while schooled families are given a pass for towing the line? I had unwittingly accepted that it was the norm to have to carry the financial burden ourselves; the boost was a much appreciated surprise and well used. We were able to buy the exact books we wanted rather than what we could find in resale shops, we had a membership to the children's science museum, and took classes such as swimming and horseback riding. I was elated to be able to provide a top quality education for my children, even while other aspects of our life were a struggle.

Lhassan and I both worked in the new-to-us business from day one, choosing it and running it together. With backgrounds working in cafes, buying a drive-thru coffee stand seemed easy enough for both of us to manage. When our newborn was six or so weeks old I returned to work in the afternoons, while Lhassan took the early morning rush and afternoon shopping shifts. I had worked soon after the birth of my other two sons, and while I would have liked to focus full-time on homeschooling my children, we had never been in a place where I could do so. It was natural to me that I returned to work, but having three children is not like having one or two. Whether we were alone or together, Lhassan and I were now always outnumbered by our children.

At shift change I would load baby and a full sized baby swing into our car and head over to the coffee shop. Lhassan would then either go home to take a nap or go straight away to replenish the daily supplies of milk, whipped cream, coffee beans, and so on with the boys in tow. Occasionally he would go shopping after I returned from the coffee shop in the evenings. Our days were tightly wrapped around running the business and caring for the children. In short time I became burnt out and frustrated by this routine. While Lhassan felt that he was carrying most of the load at the coffee shop, I felt that he had to since I carried nearly all the load at home. He was usually too tired to do any cooking let alone other housework, while I had a nursing infant and was always tired but felt there was no other way than to carry on doing what needed to be done. Quality time together was nonexistent, our communications were tense, and my frustration level was too high. One day when he was again bemoaning that I never cleaned the coffee shop floor, which I felt was far too difficult with a baby and baby swing to properly mop the narrow three by six foot space, I abruptly quit. I've had a lot of jobs over the years and I had only ever quit two others without giving proper notice. I later learned that couples who run businesses together have tragically low success rates. Whether it is the union, the business or both, something often gives.

I feel that moment, when I walked away from our business, was a definitive one in our relationship. Lhassan seemed to shut me out around that time, though I had already felt unheard and unappreciated as well as physically exhausted. Still, I felt persistent to both keep my children at home and find a way to help make ends meet. I quickly threw myself into opening an eBay shop, which I knew nothing about, but soon enough was able to contribute a little bit to our income again. I simply saw these as difficult days and did my best to stay the course. I did not feel like my husband and I were taking the same route, but I was hopeful that we would meet up again at some point.

"Flying starts from the ground. The more grounded you are, the higher you fly."

- J.R. Rim

CHAPTER SIXTEEN:
ALWAYS FORWARD, NEVER STRAIGHT

Lhassan kept the business going by himself for nearly a year before he was finally able to sell it and recoup most of the money we had put into it. It did not earn a livable wage during that time. I supplemented the income with eBay sales and help from food pantries. Even while he was plotting his next business plan, we agreed on ultimately returning to Morocco, so a move to another state wasn't a good option. Alaska is separated from the rest of the US by an enormous stretch of Canada, making the relocation from Alaska to any other state costly and complicated. We would remain in Alaska.

Lhassan, along with two acquaintances, bought a small pizza take-out shop in a fairly idle strip mall. I was opposed to the idea, not liking the partners or the location, but my counsel was no longer considered. This hurt, and again I hoped it was just a stage in the marriage. If you see it as a red flag, you are wiser than I was. I had hit a plateau with my eBay sales and needed to make a choice to continue with it, going bigger, or do something else. I was making jewelry, and working with sparkly gemstones was wonderfully enjoyable. With a little bit of research I didn't believe that the business would transfer well to Morocco, where gemstones and other supplies aren't readily available and the market would be considerably different. I knew that when we did return to Morocco, I did not want to be completely reliant on anyone else- not my husband, nor my father-in-law, nor my mother. I wanted to at least be hirable if not already gainfully employed. While I was pregnant with our fourth child I began researching and planning how to return to school and finish the degree I had left behind when I got married and pregnant in fast succession almost ten years before.

Most of my school credits were no longer transferable, which meant I would have to start nearly from scratch. But the good news was that I was eligible for grants that would cover most of my school costs. With fastidious planning, if I attended summer school, I could finish my degree in an entirely new field in two and a half years. And I did.

Looking back, I am still amazed that I was one of those women who did it all. I had four children, I homeschooled, I worked on campus, and completed a degree with exceptional grades. Lhassan was extremely supportive during this time, taking the older kids to work with him so I could get school work done or sleep with the baby. He also took on more housework... sort of.

With some of the earnings from the coffee drive-thru and help from his dad, Lhassan bought a minor fixer-upper mobile home. He was now back to regularly cooking at home and was also doing repair work when he could. I felt like we were a team again, even though we did struggle. He still no longer included me in or took my opinion about his business dealings. While he may have felt it was *his* business, I felt that how he did or didn't make money based on his sole decisions deeply affected all of us, so I should be included. Afterall, he was closely tied into how I was maneuvering my schooling and work during that time. I surely wouldn't schedule my classes in such a way that interfered with his work schedule, so he shouldn't invest his time and money in ways that I felt were too risky or undervalued. I remember being desperate to get us some couples counselling and finally found someone in California who could at least do one session with us over the phone. He was an imam (religious leader) who was also a degree-holding counselor.

It felt good to spill all my stress out to someone who would be able to review the overall picture we had sloppily shaped together and help us finesse some of the details. I told the counselor that I was overwhelmed and just wanted to plough through this period of my life so that I could be done and we could move onto the next stage. I explained as much as I could: we had four children, I was in school full-time and working part-time, Lhassan worked full-time, our children were homeschooled (meaning home and needing attention most of the day), and our income was very low meaning we got by without a lot and lived very frugally for a US lifestyle. While I understand that "busy" is the mode de jour for most people, we were far more busy than I wanted to be for any long term. Again, I saw this as a temporary state, like having your home remodeled, which oh yeah we were doing that too, but I don't know if I told the counselor that. I then bamboozled Lhassan into taking the phone call. I had told him I was looking for someone for us to talk to, but hadn't made an actual appointment for the call, I simply handed the phone to him.

I was so pleased when Lhassan and the counsellor talked for a considerable amount of time. When Lhassan finally gave the phone back to me the counsellor said, "I asked you if anything had changed from you, changed in your life..." Nothing had changed immediately, as in during the last few months, but yes our lifestyle was extremely different than it had been from when we first married, from when we lived in Morocco, from when we opened our first business - isn't life just a series of changes? I explained all of this to him, again. His response: "Your husband is unhappy about the condition you keep your house."

I simply laughed. I supposed it was better than a useless dehydrating cry session or throwing the phone at the wall. How was it that neither of these men could realize that our family was in a unique domestic position? That keeping an immaculate home simply wasn't as important to me as getting at least six hours of sleep a night, and if it was so important to the husband then why wasn't he doing more? I was somewhat relieved that this was Lhassan's only problem, and was greatly relieved just to have gotten so much off my chest even if there wasn't any resolve. Lhassan's lack of suggesting registering the kids in school may have been enough for me to consider him still supportive of homeschooling, but truly our complete lack of communication on all topics was excruciatingly unhealthy. I had an unrealistic attitude of just grin and bear it; actually I don't even grin, rather I sort of hunkered down and barreled through. I had hoped that once we got over this hurdle it would all be downhill, but the hurdles kept coming.

Living in Alaska, where there is snow on the ground more months than not, car accidents are a given whether they are your fault or someone else's. Slightly crunched SUVs festooning intersections while waiting for the police to come make a report are daily sights. I rear-ended someone within the first month we lived in Alaska. My husband finally had his accident about five years in. When his work van (the one he used to haul goods and set up equipment for his seasonal retail booth) slid off a highway on-ramp flipping onto its side, I was simultaneously thankful that he was unharmed and also felt it was a strong reminder of the impermanence of life. I was reminded that he could be gone at any second, as could I, and I needed to be able to support my family on my own. Getting our family to the position where we could have two vehicles had taken years, and in a flash we were back to one car, thankful we had that. Bussing to school and work would take hours, so instead we maneuvered complicated rideshares. I felt a new nudge of support from him as he worked with me in this vein, though it wasn't like we had pleasant chats during our frequent but brief commutes together. Then I crashed our other car.

Lhassan had bought some teenager's cute little sports car that he was going to do the needed light refurbish on and quickly flip. It wasn't intended to be driven by either of us, so he hadn't bothered to buy pricey snow tires. When I slid into the back of another car at a red light and totalled the front end of the car, I felt this was the end of everything. With my meticulously scheduled course load, if I dropped any classes, I wouldn't be able to make up any of those credits for a few semesters. A few semesters meant adding more years to hanging around Alaska, a lovely state that I still did not want to live in.

I was amazed at how Lhassan organized his friends to get us back and forth to my school and his work. In true supermom fashion, I finished my coursework the same day I went into labor with our fifth child. For whatever reasons Lhassan put in the extra effort to help me earn my degree, I remain thankful. My instincts had at least been right in one way - I would need to support myself when we finally moved overseas.

CHAPTER SEVENTEEN:
BACK NEW HOME

Within a month of earning my degree and birthing my fifth child, we were ready to return to Morocco for a much longer stay. While I had worked hard to return better prepared, and felt the husband was doing the same, we still stepped off the plane and back into the same problems. Lhassan's family business was still too messy for him to simply take on a position as promised. High unemployment rates coupled with low wages left him with few viable work options. For me... many people have this strange idea that the Americans who move overseas can simply get jobs at US embassies or "something like that". It's as if we believe that we will be catered to for simply being Americans. While there are perks and privileges to a west to east migration, I knew I wasn't going to be able to cash in on one of these rare opportunities. I had expected to slowly build up my writing career while being a homeschooling mom. I also wanted to get my master's degree from a Moroccan university and to start on that when the latest baby wasn't such a baby. Once again I felt under pressure to put any well-intended plans aside and jump in.

Our first year back in Morocco was horrible. Frankly, many repatriates and expats return to the States or Europe during their first year in Morocco or similar migrating situations, just as we had done with our first attempt at relocation. So I knew this would be a difficult period, but again you don't know what you will be hit with until you are in it. Lhassan returned to Alaska in the summer to do his seasonal work. I insisted on him doing this only one time as I didn't want to be one of the many wives I knew who were raising children alone most of the year while their husbands worked overseas. Of course there were other conditions I insisted on that fell through, but this one did not. His agreed-upon three to four-month stint in the US turned into six months. Our agreement to live in his father's cramped apartment also fell through. During this time in the first year, I went through a period of depression which finally had me getting out of bed only to go track down some antidepressants without seeing a doctor. I was desperate and broke. Some friends had sent me money, but it wasn't enough to get a legit prescription. Fortunately I was able to get them without. The fog lifted a bit, enabling me to better function during the day. Unlike our prior time in Morocco, I now had regular internet access which gave me a major boost of support from friends back home as well as making new connections locally.

I still struggled to take the kids on outings and to remain positive and active while at home. I had anticipated having our own place where we would have our own schedule and space to do all those odd activities homeschoolers love to do. Living with the in-laws was extremely limiting. While they didn't flinch at the fact that we homeschooled, they also wanted to maintain their regularly scheduled life and for us to fold around it, such as keeping specific meal and chore times. When the floors were due to be cleaned everything and everyone had to be off of them regardless of what we were doing at that time. Messy and large projects we normally did, such as composting, were an inconvenience in other people's lives. Logically I know that I'm wrong, but it felt like we had to do a lot of compromising without receiving much from the other direction. Just as I often experienced at home in the US, children and their needs are normally seen as secondary to adult needs. That just wasn't how I wanted to live, it's not what homeschooling is to me. And we were now ten people living in a two bedroom apartment. Well, eight people during the six months my husband and eldest son were back in the states.

People occasionally suggested that I put the kids in school. "They would adjust faster," was always the excuse. But would they adjust better? These kids who had never been to school, now being plunged into such an institution they had no familiarity with and didn't even speak the language - would that be best for them? I didn't believe so. I believed in homeschooling. And I still do. I continued to make the best of a bad situation.

CHAPTER EIGHTEEN:
REMOTE LIFE

An online friend lived a very unique lifestyle way out in a village in the High Atlas mountains. She boasted that now there was electricity and running water in the village, as there hadn't been when she moved there a few years earlier. I could do this, she insisted. I could give my children a truly free-range lifestyle in the mountains.

I had visited her for one day a couple of years prior. It was a ten-hour drive from Casablanca, the last three being on a winding one lane mountain road on which I was too doped up on Dramamine to fully appreciate the beauty and horror of the road which seemed to be at a continual forty-five degree angle upwards. When we pulled up to my friend's home it wasn't like the clusters of tiny rustic ram-packed earth houses we had seen along the way. It had the similar pink earth covered exterior, but was a spacious two-story home looking more like the very few luxury hotels we passed during the entire drive. Being an interior designer, her home was built to her specifications, was comfy and convenient, and had been initially designed to house travellers but was now a school she was running. With so few homes along her road, I couldn't remember any being like hers.

She sent me pictures of a modern home that while being half ram-packed earth and half cement, was "better" than the local standard which was sometimes dirt floors, sometimes without a functioning bathroom, at most with a Turkish-style toilet. Our potential new home had also been built for tourist accommodation. Somehow I convinced my husband to go see it. Even better, when he found it "not bad," I convinced him to move us there.

Once again with a newborn in my arms I threw myself into packing for another move. The moving van arrived around midnight so that we wouldn't be traveling during the hottest time of the day. The van was about half the size I had imagined, a standard eight-seater with one row of seats removed from the middle. The roof was piled high with our boxes and pinned down with netting, but still several things, including our only two bicycles, were hastily left in my in-laws garden. I wanted to be angry but was suddenly far too anxious to give it my all, and then the Dramamine kicked in and I dozed off for most of the trip.

When we did stop, I was hit by the crispness of the air. It was so clean, and high up that it nearly stung my nostrils. It was incomprehensible to me that we were standing so many thousands of feet up in the air, yet still were only on this little tiny wrinkle in the immense expanse of the High Atlas mountains which spans 1,600 miles across three countries. People think living in Alaska meant living in the wilderness. In Alaska we had Costco and every other chain retailer. Our new village didn't even have a butcher; this was something truly different for my husband and I, both happily city slickers up until then.

CHAPTER NINETEEN:
REALITY BITES HARDER FOR SOME

Roughly 8% of Moroccans live in poverty, with three-fourths living in rural communities and extremely below the poverty line. Subsistence farming, extended family living, washing clothes in natural waterways, excruciatingly limited or no use of electricity, neglected health and dental care - this is how our neighbors lived. This is to some extent how we would be living, though knowing that unlike our neighbors, we could always walk out of it. Many simply could not understand why we lived there, though appreciated when I explained that it was so beautiful and felt closer to God. I wish it was easier for me to be mindful of God at all times, but for that time being on the mountains made it easier.

Tourists occasionally pass through villages like the one we lived in. They also marvel at the immense beauty of the sage-covered mountains, the ancient walnut trees, and traditional mud-made homes seamlessly blending into the earth they were constructed of. It is a privilege to be able to pass through these areas where families have lived "so close to nature" for hundreds of generations. To live among them was a privilege few experience. For the two-and-a-half years we were there, we were the only family in the village who didn't have any blood ties to the land. This gave my children a unique opportunity to experience aspects of their Amazigh heritage and culture while remaining outsiders. We were free from many cultural restraints and my children became very free range after having been cooped up in Casablanca for two years. My boys look back at pictures of that time and wince at their bushy hair before they reminisce on all of the incredible things they did and learned.

My older children have a first-hand understanding of how people in extreme poverty live, they know real generosity and hospitality, the power and richness of nature, the true rhythm of seasons and the life cycle. They swam in watering holes, helped harvest fields, interacted with hawks, frogs, hares, donkeys, snakes, and raised rabbits. They ate simple foods, while still having access to (slow) internet and all the blockbuster movies via DVDs they stocked up on the rare occasions they went off the mountain. They had toys and art supplies, unlike their friends. We used tutors for Arabic and French, and the kids used Khan Academy online for other studies, still in an unschooling, self-led style of learning. I rarely went down the mountain as even with meds I would get car sick every time, then be wiped out for whatever tasks needed to be done and still had to get sick again to get home. The journey just wasn't worth it to me, even though I knew the breaks would do me good. Admittedly, the mountain life was more for my children than myself, but it has left an impression on me too.

You know the expression, "When the cows come home?" I didn't realize it was literal. Perhaps because when most people use it they really mean "When pigs fly." We just don't get these old time farm references anymore. Or I hope it's not just me! I thought cows were mostly like horses, they hung out in a field all day then sauntered into a barn at night. Maybe that's how some cows do it, but in our ten seasons in the mountains I learned the ebb and flow of the traditional local ways of farming and raising animals. The cows spent the days in the fields, downhill from most people's homes. The ancient aqueducts watered the fields, leaving the areas above them dry and sparsely covered with any vegetation. At sunset every night there was a lively sort of traffic as cows, goats and sheep were herded back uphill to their barns which were directly attached to or even one floor (top or bottom!) of the homes. In warmer weather the cows were tied up right outside people's front doors while goats and sheep were kept out on the mountains in handmade fenced areas. Many mornings I woke up grumbling about some child not flushing the toilet, which had to be done by dumping a bucket of water down the Turkish toilet's hole, and then I would remember I was smelling the cows who tarried five feet from my front door.

One afternoon as I had tea with some neighbors, an elderly woman told me (via my friend's interpreting) that now that I had lived there for several years I should have my own cow. While she was off about how long I had been there, I often received little quips from neighbors suggesting I was a lazy city slicker. This time I reminded the auntie that my landlord hadn't bothered to build a barn for his house and was pleased at myself for shifting the blame to his negligence. While these exchanges were fun for me, they were few. I was one of those roaming freelance workers-at-home who was often chained to my computer while the women of the village all kept a similar schedule and were able to have a regular chat. In the fall and spring, occasionally I would go for walks at sunset when many of the women were sitting in small groups carding or spinning their homemade wool. I felt like a lone writer living in an artist colony. That would have been great if I could have more easily interacted with them. Loneliness was creeping in on me.

Another downside to my country life was that Lhassan was only there halftime. As he never agreed to live there, he refused to stay longer than two weeks at a time and spent the remainder of every month at his father's home. Not only was this hard on me acting as the breadwinning parent alone with six kids for half the time, but as a woman there were many things that culturally I just could not do in the village life, such as any of the shopping. Only men attended the weekly souks where the majority of our food should have been bought. My children hated going to do this task by themselves as it was time-consuming, people tended to be less respectful to children than other adults (cutting them in line and so forth) and it was physically difficult to carry several kilos of food home from two villages away. The local shops didn't carry any produce and had very limited foods but I also wasn't supposed to go to those, so I had to rely on and fight with children to get our shopping done. I also couldn't directly pay our bills which was done in the souk's village. Our electricity was on a prepaid card which could only be refilled in the other village. If it ran out, as it occasionally did, we were out of power until someone could walk the half hour there to buy more electricity and then back. Power outages were a regular part of country life even when our card was full, as well the water would run out when the power was off. Aside from these challenges, it was draining to be so alone with my children, without other adults to help me or even converse regularly with. Even though my friend was only a twenty minute walk away, it was stressful to leave my children, not a real break to take them with me, and she had a busy life as well. The adventure wore off and it became a hard way of living, even though it was beautiful and good for those of us who were old enough to remember the experience. They may grimace at their rugged mountain stylings, but my teenagers are currently planning a trip back to the mountains to revisit their friends and the beauty.

CHAPTER TWENTY:
HOME

When I became pregnant with our seventh child, I was ready to move off the mountain. I had a promotion at work and could feasibly afford to pay more rent, but it was the extreme morning sickness that hastened my desire to move. The fatigue brought on depression and I craved an easier lifestyle, as well as access to comfort foods. Again, Lhassan and I had to argue about and then finally decide where to live. It was now my turn to make a major compromise. Rather than moving to the coastal town I had wanted to live in since I first visited Morocco a dozen years earlier, I agreed to move just outside Casablanca to be closer to my in-laws. It was mostly very refreshing to be off the mountain, to have ease of access to many things - especially the variety of foods! But it was much more expensive and living in what was essentially an affluent suburb was complicated for our large family without a car. Produce, which I love, was pricey and hard to get, all local activities were also costly and getting in and out of Casablanca was both expensive and time consuming. We were living in a basement apartment and the lack of natural light quickly brought me back down. We also only saw my in-laws a handful of times in two years, so I really didn't see the point in continuing to make the compromise. When our lease was up I insisted on moving again.

I am finally exactly where I want to be. Location-wise at least. We moved down the coast to southern Morocco, where the weather and topography is similar to what I grew up with in California. I have stunning views of the ocean from the enormous windows on the backside of my house, keeping the inside well lit throughout the day. There's a big cactus patch and soft hills can be seen in the distance on the other side of the house. We are close to a city that has many opportunities for my children and isn't hard to get to at all. As well, myself and my older kids have started a business and are developing various opportunities in the small town we live in. Food is abundant and affordable here, unlike the last two places I lived in, and I am happy with our location and lifestyle. When my older kids bemoan anything about our lifestyle I remind myself that they are teenagers and then listen again with a fairer dose of empathy.

As I type this, my divorce is pending. I have finally come to accept that my husband is content to remain in the kind of marriage we had, where he picks and chooses the support he offers. I don't want to remain in a marriage where I can't have the kinds of support I ask for. Yet still, I homeschool and I plan to continue to homeschool. Occasionally myself, my children, and others throw around the idea of at least my younger children going to school, but nothing else has changed to make that feasible. I mean, schools haven't magically become a better option than homeschooling.

Our current lifestyle is so far removed from what I had wanted and anticipated, though in some ways my hand being turned has brought it closer to aspects of my vision. I fully believe in unschooling, in child-led learning, and I have long had a fascination with the Sudbury style of schools. My far removed understanding of Sudbury, from what I've read and seen in videos, is that the children are responsible for their own education, while adults and even peers help them achieve their goals through gentle facilitation- being a sounding board to the child's plans and helping them find resources. There's no curriculum at these schools and the ages are mixed together, as is known to be far more beneficial to children than lumping them all together by age. As much as I respected the Sudbury style, you see that with my first child I was still very much in an institutionalized way of thinking, I was hands-on and seeking to control his education. As my own time and our resources have become more limited, my children have had to take more responsibility for themselves and their education.

While I currently struggle financially and emotionally, this is afterall a painful and difficult stage of our lives, the homeschooling continues and in ways I am quite proud of. The support I have gathered over the years, many of the homeschooling success stories I read hoping they could be reproduced in my own family, have come true so far. My three oldest children are pointedly working towards their goals. Two are fiercely independent, asking for my assistance rarely but when they do need it. The other is, like me, a talker and regularly pours his plans and concerns out to me, then carries on towards his goals. The younger children have a different lifestyle than the older ones did and when the boys point this out I respond by asking if they seem unhealthy or unhappy. The answer is a resounding no, but the boys still worry. That's great that they have concerns about others and that I'm not alone in worrying! My eldest two regularly do what I consider the equivalent to "peer tutoring" - doing various activities with the younger children, including taking them out to play and to tag along to their classes and tutoring sessions. My children spend a lot of time together, which was my hope when I planned to have a large family. While I pine for a supportive partner, I also see that I have a lovely family - a great deal of which resembles my hopes and hard work. My support and circumstances change all the time, this is true for most people throughout their lives. I have finally found that I am my number one cheerleader. Hearing from other members of the squad always gives me an extra lift, but I am the person I can rely on the most. When I am in down and dark moments, it not only helps me to seek out the light at the end of the tunnel, but to look back on what I have built and how my vision is panning out. At some points the vision needs adjusting, at others I just need a reminder or a reflection.

I have designed this book with the tools I use to keep myself going and to remember to enjoy and appreciate what I have and what I have done. I hope it helps you meander down your homeschooling road, stopping to appreciate the endless finger paintings and lumpy pancakes along the way.

PART THREE:
The Practical Tactical

CHAPTER TWENTY-ONE:
WELL-MEANING MOM MEMES DO NOT APPLY

I'm not so sure they are even well-meaning. A lot of those memes and shared good-parenting reminders seem aimed at preserving some sort of parenting that simply does not apply to me or most of the people I know. Mothering is not a one-size-fits-all role. What "needs" to be done in other families doesn't need to be done by your unique homeschooling family.

When yet another brilliant, yet shaming, article is passed around explaining in 800 words or less how exactly you are destroying your child's life by not reading them a bedtime story- do not click on it. When that woman, who I hope for your sake isn't one of your besties or a family-member, starts to prattle on about how proud she is that her children prefer to train for marathons than spend an afternoon staring at a screen - drown her out. Don't listen. Don't even explain yourself, excuse yourself from the conversation. Even among homeschoolers when they get into the free-range unschoolers versus classic-style debates about how your life should be scheduled (for the children's sake, of course), take it all with a huge grain of salt. There may be a few tips and tricks here and there that would be nice to implement in your life, but they are few and far between. And you have to wade through loads of guilt-inducing rhetoric for just a few gems that you can create alternatives for on your own!

I don't know what this internalized mama-guilt and shame machine is all about. Maybe we are just too overwhelmed to pause and be thoughtful; instead we regurgitate this stuff because we think it's what we are supposed to do. Whatever it is, it does not apply to you;, you have already gone above and beyond. You don't have to read bedtime stories, you don't have to eat every dinner with your family, you don't have to serve your kids a rainbow of produce everyday, and you don't have to do anything that does not work well for you and your family. As I type that, I can already hear those well-repeated rebuttals: "Sometimes we have to compromise and sacrifice, moms have to do things they don't want to..." Nope. Sure, in reality moms can be absolutely rigid, uncompromising, selfish pigs. Moms can have children for a myriad of twisted reasons, and completely neglect, abandon, and/or abuse their children. Is that you - the mom reading this book about how to successfully homeschool?

You have chosen to spend at least 25% more waking time, and then some, with your children simply by keeping them out of school. If my math is vaguely correct, this means that you can more easily fall into the trappings of putting quantity of time before quality. Apply this to parenting/mothering advice - seek out quality over quantity, a lot of that garbage just does not apply to homeschooling mothers especially. Unbelieving all those oft-repeated mama guilt trips is another area where deschooling can be an effective practice to return to again and again. It may be helpful for you to revisit "Chapter Five: Never Will I Ever Again" and note down some of the specific things you will not allow yourself to fall into being shamed for. For me, I am not ashamed that I don't read my kids bedtime stories and sometimes there are screens up on our dining table.

"We become what we repeatedly do."

- Sean Covey

"A nail is driven out by another nail; habit is overcome by habit."

- Erasmus

CHAPTER TWENTY-TWO:
HOW TO NOT DISCUSS HOMESCHOOLING

"Angry at Schools, but Protecting Schools" (ASPS) is how pioneering homeschool advocate and former teacher John Holt describes the innumerable people he encounters who know schools are problematic (even dangerous) but cannot conceptualize an alternate solution. I regularly encounter these people outside of my homeschooling circles and have finally recognized that it is not my job to help them see the alternatives. I don't need to expend energy and time educating or comforting them.

I am fortunate that most of the time when I am in a situation where I am prompted to defend my choice to homeschool, it is with a stranger. I've collected a fortress of responses to choose from depending on my mood and time allowing. For many homeschoolers this is not the case. Not only are they defending themselves in the grocery store, but immediate and extended family can either be very antagonistic to the idea of homeschooling. They may be in a culture where family members beyond spouses have legit say in the decision-making process for how their children are educated, among other things. So while I want to embrace the idea that you simply never ever have to explain yourself to anyone, that's just not true in all places at all times. There are some ways to handle (or not) these unfriendly conversations about homeschooling, and I find it helpful to have canned responses on hand so I'm not like a deer in the headlights listening to someone rant about how parents coddle their children too much these days or whatever it is they believe about homeschooling.

The Inner Circle

I have heard too many times that some wannabe-homeschooling mom isn't able to because her mom, father-in-law, a crew of family members headed by an overzealous auntie, or whoever else won't let her. Campaigns are waged, family meetings are held, votes are taken, and the child is ultimately registered in school. These moms usually held their ground all on their own or with just a husband at their side and little-to-no other support to counter all the adversity. These are tough situations. Here is my best advice, which I have been asked for under many circumstances, and through trial and error with different acquaintances and friends found to be doable:

First, don't be trapped into conversations you aren't prepared for. It is perfectly reasonable to say, "Sorry, this isn't a good time to talk about this. Let's arrange a time." And then go prepare yourself.

Gather whatever data and proof you think will best work in the scenario. What are the fears your family is facing? Lack of economic opportunity via homeschooling? The child won't be able to go to college? They think you aren't qualified to educate your child? The child's opportunities for good socialization are being questioned? Maybe it is all of these things! Make a list of the concerns, do the research to appease these concerns (thank God so many people have now been down this road before us), then either neatly compile all the answers in a document or letter, or print out the relevant studies and articles for family members to read themselves. Note: people with advanced degrees, well-known publications and former educators (who are among the biggest advocates for homeschooling) are always the best respected people to gather this kind of data from. Your audience may not be swayed by homeschool mom blogs.

Present these materials to your family before you talk to them, preferably by email or give them to your family members as you/they are leaving so that you aren't cornered into a confrontation before they have looked at the material. Keep in mind a lot of people don't actually like to read, and maybe you are dealing with truly unreasonable people who don't want to see any solid evidence in support of homeschooling. Be firm, tell them that, "I put a lot of time into finding all of this for you and I need you to read these before we can talk about homeschooling again." That's fair. Attacking you based on opinion is not fair.

Schedule your meeting, bring your notes, and it would be great if you could have another homeschooler present with you when you meet. Stick to the data and schedule another meeting if things become too heated or the facts are not being heard. There shouldn't be a rush to make such a huge commitment.

If all that doesn't work, at least you did your best, mama.

The Next Layer

With ASPS friends and family (Angry at Schools, but Protecting Schools) who don't have any real say in your decision to homeschool, yet who still like to go head-to-head with you about it, you really don't have to explain yourself at all. Seriously, *you don't have to explain your decisions to these people.* I have had plenty of people in my life who it took me too many years to recognize as haters. They would bring homeschooling into conversations not out of concern for my family or general curiosity but because they wanted to see my pain or failure. It is gross, but plenty of people are truly like that. They feel comfort in perceiving themselves as being one step up a ladder from you or anyone else. If anyone you know regularly instigates uncomfortable conversations about homeschooling, it is very reasonable - and not at all impolite - to remove the topic from the table. Women are conditioned to be polite, and when someone is not being polite in kind (such as trying to dig up some emotional dirt in our life) we often don't know how to deal with these situations. Let them know you don't want to discuss it, either specifically with them or just in general. Here are a handful or canned phrases you are welcome to use (and repeat if they try to brush past it the first time):

Let's talk about it another time.
I don't want to talk about it.
I'm talked out about homeschooling.
You can Google these questions.

Also, revisit "Chapter Five: Never Will I Ever Again" maybe there is a person here you want to never whatever with again.

Absolute Strangers

Since absolute strangers are the ones who are going to most frequently come at you (and often at the least expected or convenient times) there is plenty of need to figure out how to deal with them. After years of upsetting situations and making awkward self-defense moves I finally got to a point where I could flip people's preconceived notions with just a few words. Only once in all of my weird stranger exchanges did I encounter someone who was supportive of homeschooling; I mean other than librarians of course. Strangers are those same people who leave internet comments, they don't think before they express themselves, and they easily speak hurtful, exhausting words. You owe these people nothing. Seriously again, you do not owe strangers anything. Not your reasoning, not your time, not your energy, not a site they should totally check out, and not access to your family's private world and decision-making. You may think that you need to be a representative for homeschooling, to demonstrate the normalcy or even the benefits of homeschooling, but you don't need to be the poster-mama for homeschooling. Wouldn't that energy be better spent on your children or yourself? There are loads of witty, cutting responses you can hurl back at incredulous and uninformed strangers, but really why bother? My best response is to Keep it Simple Sweetie:

"It's unfortunate that homeschooling is so misunderstood and poorly shown in the media. It has been the best choice for my family. Byyyee."

Now that I live in Morocco, my responses are a little different. Here, most people have never heard of homeschooling and simply don't understand why an American would choose to not put her children into school. Most often people assume it is for similar reasons to why rural families commonly might not put their children in schools: because they can't afford to or don't think it's important. I have two canned responses for absolute strangers in Morocco. One: "We use an American system online" - true, my kids use the internet to get the majority of their educational curiosities fulfilled. Two: "My kids are schooled at home, like your king." The second one amuses me to no end because it is so true and how cool is that?!

The thing I wish other moms would take away from these exchanges is related to what homeschool advocate John Holt was able to pinpoint at the beginning of this chapter- these people are not sincerely concerned about your children as you may misread them to be. They know the system is deeply flawed, and they don't want to look at their own culpability for going along with the program, so they lash out at you. Do not take it to heart, it is truly about them, not you.

"Never limit oneself based on the limitations of others. If you can not inspire them - leave them to be inspired by your lead"

- Tiffany Luard

"Whilst some people inspire, others conspire!"

- Ernest Agyemang Yeboah

CHAPTER TWENTY-THREE: JUGGLING ROLES - WHAT GIVES?

My husband and I were ridiculous our first year of marriage. We wanted our home to be perfect, but with radically different styles it was difficult to agree on every piece of furniture we bought. It took us a year to find a couch we both liked. When it was delivered it wouldn't fit through the door. My husband said he would tell them to deliver "the other one we liked." I was pretty sure there wasn't another one we both liked. The next day I unwrapped an extra fluffy couch that had to be fussed with daily to maintain its plush appearance. I didn't like it then, and found its daily grooming needs especially impractical once we started having small kids who would climb around on it.

When the couch was fluffed, our home looked showroom-ready for the first few years of our marriage. It took work from both of us. Lhassan regularly cleaned all the floors (wood, linoleum, and carpet) and dealt with his couch cushions daily. Once, he was so pleased with how much brighter our townhouse seemed after he washed all the windows, otherwise who knows if I ever would have thought to do it. Windows aren't something I generally think to wash unless there may be some opaque substance obscuring my view out of them. We shared all the other domestic duties and slowly added decorative elements to the walls and higher, harder-for-children-to-reach surfaces. In the fifth year of our marriage, while we were putting together the sleigh-style frame we had finally purchased for our bed, our first son was uprooting our first plant I had also recently bought after we gave away the our others when we moved across country. Pleased with having a proper-looking master bedroom we came downstairs to find dirt and leaves strewn across the dining and living areas. This marked the beginning of the end of a showcase home for us. The steadily acquired homeschooling stuff and ongoing messy activities cemented the fully lived-in look of our home.

There are millions of tips and tricks out there to maximize your time and productivity. Being organized is a recurring theme among them. Having tried many of those tips, I still found that there simply are not enough hours in the day to deal with everything, and frankly not always enough dollars to buy all the perfect storage solutions. Excluding time spent sleeping, I really prefer to look at our days in 36 hour blocks. It's a much more spacious area to include exercise, quality time, eating all the suggested healthy foods, getting tasks taken care of - just all those things I want to get done everyday but cannot. All the things are more likely to get done in every 36 to 48 hours as opposed to just 24. It takes some of the pressure off of me to get so many things done daily.

Being disciplined and scheduled is admirable, but the results are in and achieving a healthy work-life balance is something researchers and entrepreneurs are saying is nearly impossible, and they aren't including homeschooling in their studies! Basically, we cannot have it all. People work too much, sleep too little, don't exercise and meditate/practice spirituality enough, and don't spend enough time with their loved ones. Include homeschooling into this mix and you can see the likelihood of something blowing up or someone burning out. So what gives?

For me, I have had to stop aiming for perfection in all things, and indeed there is more value in progress than perfection. As you may have guessed, the look of my home is one of the easier things for me to give up, even though the external criticisms of it have been harder for me to drown out. There is another body of memes and shaming out there directed at women and the state of our homes, and they too are hard to ignore. But you know what's harder? Keeping a clean home when there are children in it and using it all day. My house may be messy, but there are many life skills my homeschooled children have that schooled-children often are not taught. We can show our children not only how to thoroughly clean up after themselves and their projects (I love to clean as I go along, but have discovered this doesn't work for everyone), but our kids can learn how to set up a project for themselves that normally an adult might do. For instance, if there is a recipe we are going to follow, I have my children read through it and pull out everything they need before we begin. For many projects, I often hand my children my phone and have them take a photo of their set up before I begin with them so that I can let them know if anything is left out. So I give up some control (you often hear moms say they would rather do something their way than let their husband or child do it), but I gain some time to do other things for myself, and this also builds my children's confidence and independence.

The thing I most regret giving up at too many points in my adult life is exercise. While I became far too unhealthy for my comfort, I am glad to recently have made exercise a priority again as well as learning various meditation techniques. I am now practicing mindfulness (please Google it!) for a few minutes a day instead of using various media to give myself mental downtime. And please, stop praising multitasking! Multitasking is the premature killer of too many women. Focus on what is at hand only, give it 100% and the less unimportant things will have to slough off or adapt to you. Of course a great time saver is eliminating soul-sucking, energy-draining people. Is there a social circle you dread attending? Stop going. This is another dilemma of quality versus quantity. We have been conditioned to believe that there are unnamed opportunities in socializing, rather than recognizing the actual benefits of truly quality socializing. A few minutes of catch-up every now and again with a great friend/mentor is much more valuable than a weekly meet-up with people who spike your blood pressure.

One of the greatest resources for any business, and educating our kids is big business, is outsourcing. I recognized from the start that I wasn't willing to go through advanced math again, and similarly other subjects (especially languages) have come up for which it is emotionally economical for me to hire tutors. The cost of preventing my frustration and fatigue is more valuable to me than hiring a tutor. Similarly, I have a cook who keeps my kitchen tidy and prepares one healthy daily meal for my family five days a week. Even though I have worked as well as homeschooling throughout my childbearing years, it still took me nearly two decades before I met my breaking point and hired a cook. Waiting so long to hire a cook is another regret I have; her help is so much more valuable to my family than the money I spent on junk and fast food, or the far too many times I was miserable having to cook after working all day. If there is any task you find absolutely soul-sucking, think about how you can outsource it. And consider how you can do it right within your home too. My older children make pretty good pocket change washing their younger siblings' laundry.

Recognize that you simply cannot have it all, but you have so incredibly much.

Recap of Ways To Better Balance Your Homeschool-Life-Balance

1. Share the domestic workload with your partner
2. Embrace the lived-in look
3. Think beyond daily to slightly larger blocks of time
4. Recognize your progress, you do so much!
5. Do not let your health go, trade habits you feel bad about for ones that make you happy
6. Upgrade your socializing habits
7. Outsource everything you ever can, again, you do so much!

CHAPTER TWENTY-FOUR:
THE HOMESCHOOL PARENT-CHILD RELATIONSHIP

"Any child who can spend an hour or two a day, or more if he wants, with adults that he likes, who are interested in the world and like to talk about it, will on most days learn far more from their talk than he would learn in a week of school." ~ John Holt

I've heard homeschooling moms say that they keep their children out of school so they can "enjoy them" more or longer. On the surface this sounds quite greedy, but in actuality it is one of the best things about homeschooling. We have the extra time to develop loving, strong relationships with our children and truly enjoy them as the individuals they are. Quantity over quality can get in the way here, as we spend so much time with our children that we can focus too much on the academics or take the time for granted. In my home I have noticed times when we get stuck in this sort of taken for granted rut. Usually I don't realize this until one of my children begins acting adversely, and then I see that I have been encouraging this by giving too little positive or pointed attention to begin with. The parent-child relationship goes out of balance when too much time is spent in a teacher-pupil state. We have to remember to put homeschooling aside and spend quality time with our children as loving parents.

A common tactic is to spend a good chunk of mindful one-on-one time with each child once a week. I mean not educating of course, preferably doing something you both enjoy. As a mom with seven children, this doesn't work so easily for me, but I have had plenty of opportunities to see what does and doesn't work.

BE FLEXIBLE, IT DOESN'T NEED TO BE SCHEDULED, BUT THEN AGAIN MAYBE THAT WORKS BEST
Sure, it would be great to have a set date to spend quality time with your child, and while children look forward to these special times, that isn't always possible, but there are benefits to not scheduling as well. If you are easily able to regularly make one-on-one time happen with your

child, grabbing the opportunities when they arise, then it may even feel like less of a chore to both of you. It may feel more organic for both of you, as is ideal. If you are forgetful, over-scheduled, or otherwise unable to simply snatch that quality time, then scheduling may be best to ensure it happens.

MAKE THE TIME ABOUT CONNECTION, NOT MATERIALISM

Mindfulness is another key element to quality time with our children. Lunch dates are great to connect with our children, but special meal outings fall into the problem of confusing giving our children things with giving them love. Likewise taking a child shopping for other than specific needs or to a park where they will play solo aren't moments of quality time. They can give the child a mixed message that you are there as a provider (giving them things and experiences) rather than a nurturer making connections with their soul. I often take one child along when I run errands, being careful not to give into impulse purchases, and then we do usually have lunch or a snack so that I have the time and space away from the house to sit with them, but I emphasis that eating out isn't the point of this time together. Likewise I will sit with them on a bench or other public space for a bit just to be together doing not much of anything. It's not easy to actually do nothing as a means of doing quality time with your children; just be aware of the message you are giving them in the things you give them when what you want to give them is your attention.

DISCUSS YOUR INTERESTS AS WELL

Parents can fall into letting our children think that the world revolves around them and that we are essentially here to provide endless services to them. For homeschoolers this is especially tricky as we are physically on hand for our children more so than schooled-children. Let your child see you as an individual, let them know who you are. Discuss with them your interests and the things you are doing as a well-rounded adult. As a photographer, one of my favorite things to do is go through my phone's photo gallery with my children and answer their questions about the things I did or pictures I took.

Relationships with your children, like all others in your life, can go through periods of being strained. I feel that as homeschooling parents who choose to spend so much time with our children it only makes sense to put extra effort into healing these periods. I regularly seek external support to understand psychological dynamics in our relationships and to improve my communication practices with my children. This work is obviously win-win as why would we want to have cruddy relationships with the people we have chosen to spend so much time with? And they don't like to live in that discomfort either. I truly love the majority of the time I spend with my children.

AFTERWORD

As I have been writing and revising the book there are several points where I can hear readers' voices questioning my decisions. I'm used to this, but feel a closer more trusting bond with my homeschool community so I wanted to clarify just a couple of things.

I wanted to include some relationship exercises in this book, but obviously that would have been a case of 'Do as I say not as I do'. So. Please let my experience be an example of what not to do. Don't ignore the red flags, don't let regular communication with your partner lag, don't live purely on hope.

The other thing is, I wanted a large family. I am an only child and as much as I enjoy being completely spoiled, there is only one person in the world who does that for me, my mom, otherwise it can be quite lonely and tiring having to take on life's challenges all by myself. I wanted my children to have a team of supporters, especially after I am gone. I also heard that children with multiple siblings can be fairly well-adjusted, men with sisters have more empathy in general, and that most people from large families appreciate the experiences it brings. So I consciously chose to have a lot of kids, even when the timing seemed precarious. As Lhassan has said, "If we waited for the right time, we wouldn't have any of this," and I love having all of them.

Please, sister-reader, don't believe the myth about large families ruining the environment. The data repeatedly points to corporate greed being the primary danger to the environment while large families tend to be extra careful with their resources and materials. Of course, what mama of many can afford to be wasteful? I'm very happy to be raising a whole pack of people who care for our shared environment.

Brooke Benoit
January 2018

"Be you, love you. All ways, always."

\- Alexandra Elle

NOTES